Homescho
Su

How To Avoid The Battle Zone,
Motivate Your Kids
And Build The Homeschool Of Your Dreams

By

Sonya Chappell

Dedication

To my husband Rob for making homeschooling the best decision we've ever made.

To Julie Gilbert, my friend from homeschooling-ideas.com, who has taught me so much. She is my inspiration and even made this book cover for me!

To all my Facebook fans and members of the Courageous Facebook Group. Thank you for proving that homeschooling works so much better when we come together to support each other.

To Sylvia Kerslake and Joe Jenkins from authorpa.com, who have given their services for free. Thank you so much for your help – so kind of you.

And finally to my Mom, who homeschooled me all those years ago. Love you Mom.

Contents

Introduction

You are reading this because you are frustrated. You've got all these big dreams about creating a wonderful homeschool and it is **not working**.

Or you are just **starting homeschool** and want to know how to **'get it right.'**

This guide will prove to you that the biggest secret to success in homeschooling is **motivation**. If you get that right, everything else will follow.

I can show you exactly what things you can do in your homeschool to get your kids happy and enthusiastic - and what *not* to do.

Along the way you are going to learn all sorts of things about **how kids get motivated** which will blow your socks off.

Picture this:

What happens when you end up in lots of **battles** with the kids? You've had all these great plans about all the things you'll do, all the lessons you'll teach, how well they will do....and it is all falling round your ears.

The kids aren't interested. They don't want to learn.

You are tearing your hair out. This is **their future** ...Can't they realize that? What if they don't get any exams or qualifications?

They will have **failed**. And *you* will have failed too.

It is a disaster scenario.

So you try everything you can think of to **motivate** them:

- If you have a schedule, you re-jig it....yet again!
- You come up with even more ideas about how to make the subject/s interesting
- You heap on the encouragement and praise
- You explain what will happen in the future, why exams and qualifications are important
- You make tons of suggestions about what they might like to do, things they might like to try, different learning opportunities, different ways to learn
- You suggest they make more effort

And you may well try the other side of the coin - nagging/withholding privileges/shouting....You know that isn't necessarily right, but you can't help it.

Never mind. Whatever you do....
It doesn't work.

You are in a battle scenario.

The happy homes you envisaged is tumbling round your ears.

You may well find your lovely child is doing their very best to be nasty and unpleasant towards you.

Plus your partner and you are under strain - you've talked it through day after day and long into the night.

You can't make things better.

And because this is your homeschool you can't get away. You have to deal with it day after day.

And you have to **hide it** from the outside world.

Phew! Doesn't sound good does it? And there doesn't seem to be a way back.

Luckily, I am in a unique position to help you because:
- I can draw on my experience as one of the

few **second generation** homeschooling families, so I know what it felt like to be taught at home as a child **myself**

- I can use real-life insights from my **8,500+** homeschool *Facebook* fans to provide real-life insights into how they make homeschooling work for them

- I have 'succeeded' with my own kids, (at least in my terms). My son William has been accepted by **Oxford University** and my daughter is taking a very different path and following an unschooling route as an **artist**. I will use what I have learned to help make sure your homeschooling is a success too!

- I can adapt the **techniques** to homeschooling I have learned from a very inspiring free book called **'Motivating your intelligent but unmotivated teenager'** by Dennis Bumgarner. He has been counseling parents for over thirty years and has some fantastic insights into what motivation is – and isn't - which will really help guide us in our homeschooling. I borrowed the first sentence of my book from him – imitation is always the best form of flattery!

You will discover:

- The **secret** to motivating your kids

- **Practical steps** you can take in your homeschool to keep your kids motivated and in love with learning

- **Ideas** from my Facebook fans, who have been there themselves and share a range of suggestions to help you turn things round if you start facing battles with the kids

- How to deal with a potential homeschool nightmare – the responsibility of motivating your

kids through exams

- How to get back on track if you and the kids really are at **loggerheads** and all seems lost

How this guide works

- The **first part** of this guide will show you the **steps** you can take **right from the start** which will help make sure that your kids and you work happily together. It is based on our own real-life experience of success.

- The **second part** looks at how to be a successful **homeschool teacher** – and gets you to think about what being a *'teacher'* really means.

- In the **third part** we'll discover **what motivation is** – expect to be surprised! We'll use what we learn to help us if you are struggling to get your kids motivated or if you've tried - and you've lost.

- And I will prove to you that this battle is one many parents face every day with children in the **school system**. At this very moment you can be sure some parent somewhere will be shouting in exasperation: 'Get your homework done!'

N.B. I cannot guarantee these methods work for you and you follow them on your own advisement. I am assuming that you have intelligent, capable children who are simply not motivated to learn. You may need to seek professional guidance when you are homeschooling children with special needs.

Part One

How to Build a Homeschool that Motivates Children to Learn

Chapter One:

Starting Homeschooling

When the children are **young**, we start homeschooling with a massive **advantage**.

You can't stop them wanting to learn!

Everything is interesting. The way the beetle crosses the path, counting Lego, naming the colors.

You are on a roll. Your kids are motivated. You are motivated.

As my homeschooling icon John Holt says:

"It is hard not to feel that there must be something very wrong with much of what we do in school, if we feel the need to worry so much about what many people call 'motivation'.

*A child has no stronger desire than to **make sense of the world**, to move freely in it, to do the things that he sees bigger people doing."*

~ John Holt

And if you're worried about what it means to homeschool, take a look at these reassuring words from Janet:

"You don't need a lot especially at the start. Take him out, give him chance to recover and see where his curiosity takes him - you'll be amazed; I know I was."
~ Janet

That makes homeschooling **easy**!

Well, maybe not.

Because, although your young child is pre-programmed to want to learn, new homeschoolers are pre-programmed to **worry**!

You will undoubtedly face homeschooling challenges.

After all, because you are doing something different from other parents, you feel **vulnerable**.

But usually, especially if you children haven't already been to public school, your kids motivation isn't the problem.

*"At least, the standard developing children... but I think that not too few families decide to homeschool their not standard developing children... and some of them may have **lack of curiosity**, among other*

signs of not standard development..."
   ~ Maria

So don't beat yourself up if your child needs more help to find what calls to them.

Plus, if you are taking your kids out of school to start homeschooling, you may well find you need quite a period of **de-schooling** before those natural interests begin to re-surface.

It is quite common in those circumstances to have to wait **six months to a year** or longer before your child starts to show renewed enthusiasm.

And I've also heard Mom's say they need a period to de-stress and de-school themselves!

Once you've got over that hump, your child will begin to re-discover their natural joy of learning.

As **Maria Montessori** discovered all those years ago:

"Education is not something which the teacher does, ...it is a natural process which develops spontaneously in the human being."
   ~ Maria Montessori

That takes a lot of the burden off your shoulders – because your child will lead the way in teaching themselves what they need to know.

"Follow your heart! I wouldn't buy a thing for now ...When he finds an interest in something be resourceful and use your imagination, the internet is our best friend and its amazing what you can find for free/cheap when you look for it."

~ Bettie

"Learning is part of their nature, you couldn't take it off them even if you wanted to."

~ Leyli

Homeschooling gives you the unparalleled opportunity to give your child the love and individual attention they deserve to uncover their unique talents and abilities.

You can't hurry the process, but you can **rely** on most children **wanting to learn.**

So when does that start to change?

That's vital to discover, because once your kids enthusiasm for learning is gone, it is game over as far as homeschooling is concerned.

Chapter Two:

Why Does Homeschooling Fail?

This book answers the biggest nightmare of all when it comes to homeschooling:

Battles with the kids.

Why is that the biggest and most important threat to creating a successful homeschool?

Because you are a **parent first** and foremost.

Your main role is to offer a haven which your child can turn to for **love, comfort** and **acceptance.**

If your child finds a subject boring and she is playing up, it is the teacher who takes the brunt.

But if you are homeschooling, it is Mom (or Dad) whose dealing with the fact that the last essay looks like a spider just crawled across the page.

Homeschool is **one-to-one** and you are a parent. This isn't a teacher with a class.

And the most important thing is to keep a **loving, close, relationship** with your child.

If you start having daily battles over work stuff, well, quite frankly, **you'd be better off sending your child to school**.

So if you can't motivate the children to learn, you are up the creek without a paddle.

Now, obviously there are other problems you have to deal with when you are homeschooling.

They include:

- your own worries and **fears** about **failure** and whether you are '**good enough**'
- the difficulty of being an adult **alone with the kids** for much of the day
- linked to that, lack of your own status and loss of **self-confidence**
- feeling you haven't the **knowledge** to teach certain subjects
- **outside pressure** from relatives and society
- worries about your child's **socialization**

You'll find lots of useful techniques to help you

overcome these fears and succeed in the free *Courageous Homeschooling course* on my website at *www.homeschool-activities.com.*

The free **Courageous Homeschooling e-course** covers:

- **techniques** to build your confidence
- **research** to prove that homeschool kids are often better 'socialized' than their school fellows
- **reassurance** that you are the best teacher your child could hope for
- and....lots more!

But this guide will reveal to you that the biggest path to success in homeschooling is **motivation**. If you and your kids can work happily together, everything else will follow.

Let's begin by taking steps right from the start so you don't sow the seeds of self-destruction in your homeschool.

Chapter Three:

Homeschool Scheduling

How you organize your homeschool is a very significant factor in whether you **kill off** your kids desire to learn.

Homeschool 'success' isn't guaranteed just because your children are little.

Your homeschool will still have its **ups** and **downs**.

You may well join the rest of us in worrying about whether your child will **'keep up.'**

(Secretly, of course, hoping you'll soon be able to boast how far **in front** your child is now you are homeschooling!)

So you start introducing **scheduling** and

workbooks. Things which **have to be** 'learned.' Like Math, reading and writing.

Maybe you have no choice. State regulations require it.

Does that kill your child's motivation?

I don't think so.

Scheduling can really help some children who like order and knowing when things are. And, more importantly, you have to do what suits **you**.

It is no good trying to be free and easy and go with the flow if it is driving you nuts!

Mostly I think you won't have a problem with introducing a schedule - at least at first.

- Your child is **young**; they want to learn.
- You will be more **flexible** - there'll be plenty of 'non-work' times in the playground, reading with Mom, doing the garden, playing with friends.

And I'm sure you will be doing your best to help by making your set time learning interesting by trying to find the best curricula and looking out projects and activities which your child can do which are both fun and tick the boxes.

Moreover, as you begin to **relax** as a homeschooling parent and see your children growing and learning in all sort of ways, generally your scheduling relaxes too.

BUT there are some very important points in all this which is I think one of the secrets I can now see to why our homeschool was successful.

- We **involved the children** in making the schedule.
- Even when they were very little, we would all agree roughly **when things** would happen.
- We did projects around the childrens' **interests.**
- We built in time that was **special time just for them** to use anyhow they chose - so long as they were relatively quiet!

The point is: if you get your children to sign up to the schedule they are far more likely to be **motivated** to follow it.

Here's Sheila to give that idea a thumbs up:

*"I'm starting to sit down and **plan the day with her** so she feels more in control and will follow 'her' plan more willingly."*

~ Sheila x

So your battles will be far less. And, just like with parenting, the more you can agree to doing things your child **wants to do**, the better.

*"The fact is that given the challenges we face, education doesn't need to be reformed -- it needs to be **transformed**.*

*The key to this transformation is not to standardize education, but to **personalize it**, to build achievement on discovering the individual talents of each child, to put students in an **environment** where they **want to learn** and where they can naturally discover their true passions."*

~ Sir Ken Robinson, International Educationalist

(who gave the most popular TED talk ever on *Why Schools Kill Creativity* – do watch it!)

Chapter Four:

Choosing A Schedule

Some parents follow a **school-at-home** approach.

I have a friend who set up a blackboard in one room and had each of her five children sitting at desks.

There wasn't a bell or a uniform - but otherwise it was as similar to school as it is possible to make it.

That system suited the parent. She had been a teacher in public school and it made her feel good to show everyone else how brilliantly she was teaching compared to all her colleagues.

It is a perfectly reasonable choice.

You have to do both what suits you and also what you think **suits the children**.

I was one of the first homeschool children taught by my pioneer homeschooling parents and they used much more of a **traditional school approach**.

I LOVED being homeschooled. That's why I decided to teach my own children at home myself.

BUT there is a **problem**.

If you set up a system like this you are likely to run into more battles with the kids.

What happens when someone doesn't do their homework? When they won't complete an assignment? When it hits 10am and they are still on break?

That's something you need to think about before you pick your method.

Plus, you need to choose your schedule according not only to what suits you best, but also what learning style suits your children best.

I thought this was very interesting:

*"Richard Felder is co-developer of the Index of Learning Styles. He suggests that there are **eight different learning styles**.*

- ***Active** learners absorb material best by applying it in some fashion or explaining it to others.*

- **Reflective** *learners prefer to consider the material before doing anything with it.*

- **Sensing** *learners like learning facts and tend to be good with details.*

- **Intuitive** *learners like to identify the relationships between things and are comfortable with abstract concepts.*

- **Visual** *learners remember best what they see, while*

- **Verbal** *learners do better with written and spoken explanations.*

- **Sequential** *learners like to learn by following a process from one logical step to the next, while*

- **Global** *learners tend to make cognitive leaps, continuously taking in information until they "get it."*
~ Sir Ken Robinson

That sounds potentially a bit confusing, especially if you are catering for the different needs of eleven children, like my homeschool friend Rachel.

But the point is....you can expect your schedule to change as you work out more clearly the **best-fit** approach for all of you.

Look at what Sharon says:

"Homeschooling gives you the freedom to teach your children according to their individual learning styles. In a traditional school setting, you don't get that. They have to teach many students, and sadly, many children are unable to thrive in that

environment."
~ Sharon

Some of us choose a mix of scheduled time and **unschooling**, where the kids do their own thing and direct their own learning.

"We don't do 'school work'. Simple." ~ Gail

*"We have days where we do no work but the rest of the time have a **scheduled** approach. I go with the flow."*
~ Sheila

"The thing I like most is that we are free to work along our own schedules. I really disliked having to take my child in 5 days a week at set times. Some days I just wanted us to do something else and enjoy each other's company when he was not tired from a whole day at school!
Life is too short to give your children up to others to be raised!"
~ Saadiya

If you decide to **unschool**, you are letting the kids decide **when** and **what** they want to learn.

Which means they are responsible for their own motivation and you aren't badgering them to do things they don't want to.

Here's a really interesting quote from Hazel from my Courageous Homeschooling Facebook Group:

*"Been unschooling my 12 year old for a couple of years since **the agonies of structured learning** for her. No formal English or Math. I do panic sometimes (actually quite a lot), but she has taught herself things she is interested in from YouTube, especially wedding type hairstyles which she is amazingly talented in, and we read loads of good living history etc. type books. ...*

*Now, **if I could just get school out of MY head** I'm sure I would feel better and be more supportive of her. I find that lots of physical activity helps too. My 7 yr old does some structured stuff but I find that it is for me really as she has learned a lot independently. I think the danger with set work (for us) is that they think they have "done" school and natural learning takes a nose dive."*

~ Hazel

There's lots of useful stuff in here for all of us.

It raises all sorts of questions about what makes your child want to learn, and how structured learning **can** be a problem.

To most outsiders, the idea that the kids will learn **by themselves** seems totally **irresponsible**.

Except that research is increasingly proving that with all the learning opportunities lying around in a fairly affluent house you, the parent, don't actually need to **do** much.

Here's John Holt to explain:

"(My work) will be a demonstration that children, without being coerced or manipulated, or being put

*in exotic, specially prepared environments, or having their thinking planned and ordered for them, **can, will and do** pick up from the world around them important information about what we call the Basics.*

*It will also demonstrate that **"ordinary" people**, without special schooling themselves, can give their children whatever slight assistance may be needed to help them in their exploration of the world, and that to do this requires no more than a little tact, patience, attention and readily available information."*

~ John Holt

Let's take a few examples from my Facebook fans to see what unschooling looks like in real life:

*"We don't have any **formal lessons** unless they ask for them - apart from a few times recently when I've got them to do an activity because I've decided to (on and off over the last few months for my 10 and 9 year olds).*

*But I make sure the environment that they're in has lots of **learning opportunities** (most do!) and we'll look for the ways to learn - the fun game, good read-aloud, interesting conversation, new place to visit, etc. "*

~ Katie

My proviso is that, even with unschooling, I think it is very important to take the time to encourage your child's natural interests – which I'm certain you are doing.

*"We have to go from what is essentially an **industrial model** of education, a manufacturing model, which is based on linearity and conformity and batching people. ...We have to recognize that human flourishing is not a mechanical process; it is an **organic process**.*

And you cannot predict the outcome of human development. All you can do, like a farmer, is create the conditions under which they will begin to flourish."
~ Sir Ken Robinson

The surprising thing is that **even if you back off** your child will probably be way ahead of their peers in many areas, at least until you hit High School age.

You just have to be relaxed about the things **they can't do**.

That's something a school can't afford to do. It has to keep all the kids learning at roughly the same rate so that the teacher can manage a large group of kids at the same time.

"Many schools are organized as they are because they always have been, not because they must be."
~ Sir Ken Robinson

Look at this very interesting quote from Will Richardson (you'll hear more from him later!)

*"We know that separating learning into discrete subjects and time blocks is **not** the best way to prepare kids for the real world. School is the only place in the world where we do math for 45 minutes, and then science for 45 minutes, and then Shakespeare for 45 minutes.*

That's an efficiency that serves the system, not the students."

~ Will Richardson

Unschooling, on the other hand, is a method that fits common sense: we all learn differently, at different times and different rates.

In public school, not being able to **write** until High School age would be considered a matter of serious educational concern; William, now going to Oxford University, proves that if you are homeschooled it is not the slightest hindrance.

But I'm not trying to advocate that the only way to have motivated kids is by **unschooling**.

That's your choice.

We are a surprisingly long way off understanding and accepting how children actually learn.

We still need to see visible 'proof' that the child is doing something.

And it may well drive you bonkers seeing your

child on the i-pad/i-pod/i-phone/laptop or equivalent all day.

I certainly struggled with that.

I needed to see us **doing 'things'**.

Maybe that was a failing of mine.

All I can say is that in terms of motivating your kids to learn - if you aren't asking them to do set learning activities then you certainly won't be having battles over them!

Which doesn't mean that there won't be battles over behavior, but that's entirely down to your own parenting, what you feel comfortable with - and well beyond the scope of this guide.

I believe the method you choose is really up to you and **what suits your child** and **your family** best.

All methods are paths that can lead to homeschooling success.

"If your children can read and write - however little - are polite, kind and will follow instructions, if they want to learn about the world, then they are already on a level with a lot of adults and they will find their way in life."
~ Janet Xx

But there are four things that **massively reduced** the battles in the way we organized our homeschool which you can use to help you.

Chapter Five:

Scheduling Secrets

Secret One:
Flexibility

Think about it. If you are not in the MOOD to clean the fridge, you aren't going to want someone else telling you to do it.

Some days you just don't FEEL like doing things.

It is exactly the same with kids. Though hopefully you have planned something a bit more exciting to do!

They have moods too.

So if it is obvious that the lesson isn't going well, I strongly suggest you take a rain check whether it is on your schedule or not.

That way you aren't winding up the **lack of motivation** spring.

In a way, the signs that it is a bad time are usually pretty obvious with kids.

What's more of a lesson is that it can well be the wrong time for YOU too!

We sort-of assume that because we are the adult we should be able to perform equally well every single day. In reality we get tired, short-tempered and nasty ourselves!

So give yourself and your kids a chance; cut down those battles by being flexible whatever schedule you choose to follow.

A lot of homeschooling is about having the courage to follow common sense.

A common sense that flies in front of much of what society currently does!

After all, we all know really that when we go to work Monday to Friday there are some days we work really really well and other days - well, it is a waste of time showing up.

So give yourself a break. Be kind on the kids and on yourself.

Secret Two:
Work Outside

Mom had six children, most of whom were homeschooled at various points.

If you ask her how she coped, her answer would be surprising.

She got us outside!

And, if you read my interview with her in my free ***second generation homeschooling serial***, you'll see she says something fascinating:

"I considered **walks in the country** to be a large part of your **education**."

Just as well the Inspector didn't know what I was doing half the week!

I am a firm believer in the amount of **real learning** you get from doing as many outdoor activities as you can.

Going for a walk in the woods does something BIG for the mind which, at present, is beyond our understanding to quantify.

Richard Louv, the international best-selling author, is just one professional who believes that children are suffering from Nature Deficit Disorder, causing obesity, attention disorders and depression.

*Research shows that exposure to nature reduces **children's stress levels** by **up to 28%.***

And there's another plus in terms of motivation.

Kids **love** being outdoors!

The energy bounces off them in a way that just doesn't happen when they are cooped up indoors.

Those shouts and screams drift harmlessly away in the wind.

You all get less wound up. Plus, battles with the kids usually seem fewer and easier to deal with when you are outside.

So why not take advantage of that when you are homeschooling?

Nature walks are the tip of the iceberg.

Once you put your mind to it, it is surprising just how much homeschooling you can do in your **back yard**!

You can easily transport many curriculum activities **outdoors**.

How about some of the projects you will find on my website, like making blood with jelly beans, water painting, marbling....they're all ideal as things to do in the fresh air.

And the big bonus is:

You don't have to worry about the carpet!

Secret Three:
Try working with other families

Now I know this can have it is own problems and you need to weigh up the pros and cons for yourself.

Homeschool groups can be **fantastic**.

Apart from the socialization factor, some groups organize learning activities, guest speakers, art competitions, group outings and museum visits.

Our local group even has tutors to teach older kids exam subjects and gets funding to help pay for exams.

I got a lot out of going to homeschool groups.

It is great being able to unwind in the kitchen over a cup of coffee after a **hard week** with the kids.

And it is such a relief to be with people who understand, and where you can **drop your guard** without needing to justify your decision to homeschool.

As for William and Catherine, they definitely got something from it, though you'll see I think the socialization aspect of homeschooling has been blown out of proportion and lots of us waste far too much time worrying about it.

In any case, homeschool kids are like all kids - they aren't all guaranteed to be **nice**!

Similarly, homeschool **groups** are like all groups - full of dynamics where you can spend all your time and energy trying to fit in and sometimes get very **hurt** in the process.

What worked best for us was to choose another family where we all 'clicked' and have a weekly science lesson together.

The benefits are:

- It is a change of routine.
- The kids are less in your face and you are less in theirs.
- There is a high motivation among the adults to work together to make sure all the kids are enjoying themselves.

So it can be a **win-win** for everyone.

Secret Four:
Don't be too rigid on 'Targets'

Now I know you may have State targets to meet.

My advice would be: if you can and it is possible to get away with it, use all your experience as an adult to obfusticate to cover up where your child is 'behind.'

Once you get yourself tuned in, it is generally easy to learn all sorts of *education-speak* to cover any activity you do so it sounds educational.

It is a definite skill but one teachers are trained in!

For example, a trip to the **library** becomes:

- *research instruction, silent, sustained reading, resource identification.*

Legos/K'Nex becomes:

- *fine motor skills, design, math (counting), building critical thinking, logic skills.*

And **family chores** could be:

- *life skills, manual skills, economics, time-on-task development, values education.*

In other words, you don't need to write down only the things that are obviously 'educational' and you can hide a lot of other things behind it.

Once you start learning the rules of the game life becomes so much freer for all of you.

My Mom got very good at it!

The reason is this:

Common sense tells us that everyone learns at **different rates** and **different times**.

And one of the main advantages of homeschooling is that you can give your children time so they learn **when they are ready**.

This is vital in terms of motivation.

"A FEW YEARS AGO, I heard a wonderful story, which I'm very fond of telling. An elementary school teacher was giving a drawing class to a group of six-year-old children. At the back of the classroom sat a little girl who normally didn't pay much attention in school. In the drawing class she did.

For more than twenty minutes, the girl sat with her arms curled around her paper, totally absorbed in what she was doing. The teacher found this fascinating. Eventually, she asked the girl what she was drawing. Without looking up, the girl said, "I'm drawing a picture of God." Surprised, the teacher said, "But nobody knows what God looks like." The girl said, "They will in a minute."

~ Sir Ken Robinson

If you are trying to push them to write before they want to, the battles will begin.

I still remember William crying so hard as he tried to write his *Thank You* letter the ink might as well have been invisible.

We all make mistakes, me included.

I felt **vulnerable** about teaching the children at home, especially with my in-laws.

So having a nicely written *Thank You* letter was very important **to me**.

It was a visible sign to the grand-parents: Look how well William can write – see aren't we doing well!

The fact that William hated writing and could hardly hold the pen didn't come into my thinking.

I tried all sorts of suggestions to interest him in writing - letter codes, stories, cartoons, shopping lists - the only thing that worked were lists of parts for his dinosaur robots.

Luckily, I came to my senses. I could see he was getting really upset.

So I pulled back. And later I read a lot of research to show that boys are generally much slower at learning fine motor skills than girls.

He couldn't really write until High School age.

It was embarrassing for me – and it would have been **intolerable** if he had been in school.

But by waiting until he was ready we avoided the arguments, didn't put him off writing and he can **now write** – not brilliantly I have to say – but perfectly acceptably.

Which comes to another problem with targets.

Don't set the bar too high!

Expectations on yourself and your kids can really kill homeschooling.

All the research proves the academic advantage of teaching your child at home.

But it is not magic.

And you need to watch out that, just like me, you aren't going for the **reflected glory** of having a child who can perform beautifully so you can prove how brilliantly **you**, the homeschooling parent, are doing!

You'll soon find the problem with hitting targets is that they are **artificial markers**.

They have been designed by adults to measure performance.

They are not **tailored** to your child.

*"I have **no interest** in my children "progressing **at the same rate** as public school children." I understand the research and it is good to have that research. Yet, I want more for my children like to be allowed to progress at their rate which often means **asynchronous** learning.*

*In other words, they may score way above grade level in English (and I only know this because NC requires yearly testing) and below grade level in math. And **I am OK** with that."*

~ Gina

When you think about it, who cares **when** your child learns to write so long as they can do it at some stage and it isn't holding them back?

*"It is just a suggestion but I sometimes found that I set my homeschool goals way **too high** and sometimes I couldn't think of many at all.*

*Nowadays I start by asking my son and we talk it through and **set them together**."*

~ Samantha

It is a bit like potty training. At the time it seems terribly important that your child is like all other children and doesn't wet themselves.

It can be seen as a reflection of your parenting.

But once your child is potty trained everyone forgets about it.

This is a hard one as a homeschool parent.

There's nothing worse than some relative asking you:

'Can she read yet?'

So you have to stay strong.

And you also have to avoid the temptation to **compare** your children to other kids. It doesn't matter if your son's seven-year-old friend knows all of her times tables, or the eight-year-old down the street is already writing script.

Homeschooled kids have the luxury of learning when **they're ready to** learn.

And I would allow yourself to take advantage of a get-out clause because a bit of tactical white-lying, changing the subject and general misleading is perfectly acceptable too!

"Childhood is not a race to see how quickly a child can read, write and count. Childhood is a small window of time to learn and develop at a pace that is right for each individual child."

~ easypeasykids.com.au

All these are things to think about when you come to work out what sort of schedule to have - or whether to have one at all.

But the secret behind all the success is that you need to watch out for signs that your child is becoming resentful and **switched off**.

In that case, a re-think of your schedule may well save you from more battles to come.

Because the problems start when you are trying to push things on your child **they don't want to do**.

Part Two

How to Be
A Successful
Homeschool Teacher

Chapter Six:

Teaching Styles

Even more important than what sort of schedule you end up with is how you teach.

Because when you choose to homeschool, there is an elephant in the room.

And that's you.

You are the parent. But now you are the **teacher** too.

That is potentially an enormous problem on the motivation front.

When your child goes to school, the teacher/pupil battles are mostly outside the family.

Obviously that isn't entirely true because, as we'll see, many many parents struggle with motivating their children.

All parents worry about schoolwork, homework, what the teacher's say, school reports, etc etc.

But at least you are not actually teaching your child directly. That's **someone else's responsibility**.

Now you are homeschooling ---- well, welcome to the challenge zone.

Because the model that comes into your mind of being a 'teacher' is the one you probably have from your own experience of being at school as a pupil.

It is obvious isn't it?

You stand at the front and you teach. You know all the answers. You keep order. The children behave.

And it all works like clockwork.

Hmmmm.......

The reality is that teachers are put into a system which dictates that they have to deal with:

• Teaching a **large** (generally too large) **group** of children.
• Making sure all those children are learning the **same thing** at the same time.

- Having to follow a **curriculum** that they themselves don't necessarily want to teach.
- Keeping **order** and instilling discipline.

In order to deal with that, teachers need to use skills which aren't necessarily pleasant - like putting kids down, showing people up, and using **punishments** as well as rewards.

That is NOT the same situation as you face as a teacher at home.

Either you'll be teaching **one-to-one** with your child or you'll have a family of **children** of **different ages** and you'll be trying to work out how best to meet all their different needs.

(Which is a challenge in itself! One of the most common questions I get asked is how to homeschool children of mixed ages...)

Now, in terms of motivation, in some ways you have **massive advantages** as a homeschooler.

First of those is:

You can teach according to your **child's interests**.

I can't tell you just how much of a **gift** that is.

*"I want my children to love to learn. Learning shouldn't be torture and painful. If you want them to be life-time learners, you've got to let them do **what interests them**. When they want to learn, they will learn, and you won't have to make them do anything. They'll be inspired and excited.*

Find their passion and talents, then you'll have to make them stop!"

~ Dayna

You'll be amazed just how much of the curriculum you can cover if your child is interested in space, or animals, or arts and crafts, or playing music...

And they won't even notice they **are** actually covering - and often far exceeding - the **targets** set by a more conventional curriculum.

There are tons of exciting projects and homeschool activities to choose from which feed your child's curiosity.

You are not going to face many motivation problems if your child loves animals and you are doing a project on Big Cats!

*"(In school) we continue to focus our efforts primarily on content knowledge...If we would acknowledge that **true learning** is **unforgettable**, made of the the things that we want to learn more about, we'd radically shift our focus."*

~ Will Richardson

But it is not just about WHAT you teach that's important.

It is HOW you teach.

Chapter Seven:

The Homeschool 'Teacher'

Being a teacher at school is **top down**. The kids aren't expected to come up with their own ideas - unless it is in a context that's already pre-determined.

And I think schools would tend to agree that their method tends to **knock the motivation out** of the children.

That's not so much of a problem because schools have methods in place to deal with that.

Not only do they have their own tried and tested techniques of reward and punishment, they also have the benefit of **peer pressure**.

If all the kids in the room are doing something, it is much harder to say NO.

So the motivation comes from being in a group of peers who are all doing the same thing.

Schools and teachers then spend the later years of High School trying to re-instill the motivation the system has knocked out of the children when they were little.

They admit that; they know that actually their methods **don't work** in the **long run**.

"Education is the system that's supposed to develop our natural abilities and enable us to make our way in the world. Instead, it is stifling the individual talents and abilities of too many students and killing their motivation to learn.

*There's a huge **irony** in the middle of all of this."*

~ Sir Ken Robinson, International Educationalist

We all know that higher education depends on self-motivation; the students have to get on with things themselves because they **want to**.

So suddenly when the kids hit late High School age there's a turn around at school.

Amazingly, the teachers are having to begin to teach their pupils **how to learn** because they've just spent the last fifteen years bashing the spark out of them.

Rob and I had a silent chuckle when the School

Principal announced at William's new school that teacher's would be on hand to help the pupils begin 'self-directed' learning.

Just stand back and watch little children - they'll show you what self- directed learning looks like before it is trampled on!

So that again teaches us a lesson that's crucial when it comes to homeschooling.

All true learning is only possible because the child **owns** that learning. The teacher can bang on about something as long as they like.

It is the child who actually determines whether they are going to learn anything or not.

(Homeschooling) "is about raising the child you had, not the one you thought you'd have. It is about understanding they are exactly the person they are supposed to be. And if you are lucky they might be the teacher who turns you into the person you are supposed to be."
~ adapted from: *The Water Giver* by Joan Ryan

So that's a relief.

You don't need to be the EXPERT. You don't need to know everything.

So if you are asking yourself: *Can I do*

homeschooling? you might just as well say: *Can I be a parent?*

The analogy is remarkably apt.

If you set up a committee to decide on all the mothering and fathering skills you'd need – *Wow!* that's guaranteed to make you feel overwhelmed.

But look at everything you've achieved already.

Whatever the age of your child when you consider homeschool, you've already past the hardest test.

Just look at all those things you've already **taught**.

I use the word aptly.

Your preschool activities would undoubtedly have included important social skills like fairness and taking turns.

You will also have taught an amazing number of academic subjects like math using fun kids math activities without even thinking about it.

What about all those books in bed? Counting cuddly toys? Helping build Lego sets and marble runs?

So what are the **essential skills** you need as a homeschool teacher?

You need to be:

- Patient
- Able to listen and answer honestly (including saying when you **don't know**)
- Inspiring, so the child wants to **find out for themselves**
- Interested in what your child tells you
- Kind
- Encouraging

Bingo! You have it. Exactly the same sort of skills that go to make a good parent.

What's more, most teachers would give their eye teeth to be able to teach one-to-one as much as you can when you homeschool because they know that's by far the most **efficient** way to learn.

That's why all the research proves the academic advantage of homeschooling.

Expertise, knowledge of a particular subject area, is far less important than the skills you already possess to help your child acquire that knowledge.

Teaching is really about lighting the touch paper and standing well back.

If you can awaken an interest in your child so they **want to learn**, they will.

The well-known psychologist Peter Gray puts it well:

"We are so stuck on the idea that children must be forced to learn that we can't even imagine that a child might be better off learning without being forced."

~ Peter Gray, PHD

If you really think you don't know a subject well enough to teach it, you do know how to find out the answers and you can work with your child to find them.

"This commitment allows your family to choose **what** *and* **how** *your precious child will learn. You will be going back to school too. Some days you will be sure you have lost your mind. Then, suddenly you will be standing at their graduation ceremony wondering how it went by so fast.*

If the family is in agreement, it is the best, if not the biggest, investment that could ever be made on behalf of the children. I am so thankful we are a homeschool family."

~ Tes

Chapter Eight:

YOU as Teacher

I think the BIGGEST secret of our homeschool success was in the **manner of our teaching**.

You have to LEARN WITH your child.

Your role is above all to help and encourage. NOT to lead and to tell.

I would go so far as to say that this approach is so different from the **typical school teacher** that it is actually a **disadvantage** to have been one yourself.

If you are the sort of teacher who loves to stand in front of the class and give a sort of **performance**, your class will probably love you.

They certainly loved my Dad.

He was so good at motivating the class that he was always given the hardest to reach and most switched-off young people in the college to teach, like bricklayers and plumbers.

Despite having been to Oxford University himself, he believed that the **education system fails** most people....which is why later on he decided to work with prisoners.

But, although Dad was a brilliant teacher, he wasn't cut out for a structured homeschool approach.

He didn't have the patience for **one-to-one**. The **frustration** would have got to him – which is why when he homeschooled his two young sons he left them pretty much to do what they wanted.

Needless to say, they both turned out fine!

I am not into teacher bashing. For one thing many of my relatives and best friends are teachers!

And I know that most teachers are **totally committed to the children** and trying to do their very best.

Number Two on the Washington Post's list of the twelve qualities great teacher's share is:

Love of kids.

That's something to be proud of.

It is a career which attracts committed, conscientious, people who are trying to help children.

It is the **system** that's the problem, not the individuals.

How many children come out of school saying that such and such a subject is **BORING**? How many children end up as adults with **NO interests**?

William got his A*s largely because he taught himself. Chemistry is NOT my strong point!

Neither, to be honest, is Physics or Astronomy, so I passed those over to Rob who knew enough to act as an 'enabler.'

Yet if you said to a teacher that a child who is motivated can largely teach themselves I don't think they'd believe it!

And the fact that the system fails so badly in motivating so many children is absolutely proven.

For many children, it doesn't even work in a school setting.

It certainly ISN'T going to work at home.

"Some of the most brilliant, creative people I know did not do well at school.

Many of them didn't really discover what they could do—and who they really were—until they'd left school and recovered from their education."

~ Ken Robinson

When they are little, you may get away with playing teacher.

As your kids get older, it will get increasingly hard.

Because, sadly, there is another fact to face:

Most exam work is BORING.

We'll...errr...examine (!) this a bit more in the Part Three, when we look at motivation problems.

Let's conclude by acknowledging that, as a homeschooling 'teacher', you need to throw the school model of your role out of your mind.

Teachers at school have little choice, they have to short cut the process of learning because they have no time to sit and stare.

The best approach to teaching when you homeschool is much more of a **'we're all in this together'** attitude.

I'll borrow some lines from Robert Frost because he puts it better than I can:

"I am not a teacher but an awakener."

~ Robert Frost

You may know the answer, but you are the helper who is guiding your child to want to find out for themselves.

It is the seed that gives your child the internal motivation which successful homeschooling relies on.

"We're not trying to do 'School at home.' We're trying to do homeschool. These are two entirely different propositions.

We're trying to cultivate a lifestyle of learning in which learning takes place from morning until bedtime 7 days each week."

~ Steve and Jane Lambert, *Five in a Row*

Chapter Nine:

Helpful Teaching Hints

Hint One

It really helps if you can get a **real interest** yourself in the subject. Find something out about *space* that YOU never knew.

Learn how to make a volcano explode, put glo sticks in the bath, build a lava lamp - they're all fun for everyone!

Now, I know not everything is interesting – especially when the kids are little.

A friend of mine, who had just found out she was expecting another baby, confided in me that the thing she dreaded most was having to face the *Playmobil* stage all over again.

Shame, because I love the set with the bunnies in the hutch!

But the point is that, even though you can *play* at it, you are **an adult**!

So you are likely to get bored at some point however hard you pretend otherwise.

I have lots of suggestions for how to stop your mind wandering in the free Courageous Homeschooling Course on my website.

But what I would say is that planning homeschool activities which motivate and encourage all your family members is a test which requires full-on brain power!

Thinking up a day like that certainly called on all the skills and intelligence I previously needed as a Company Director.

It is not an easy thing to do.

But very rewarding when it works!

Hint Two

I also found it very helpful to have a project where the children could do what they wanted – like draw dinosaurs - while **I set myself the same task** but I did it as an adult.

Children learn SO MUCH from watching adults

doing things.

Here's John Holt:

"I think children need much more than they have of opportunities to come into contact with adults who are seriously doing their adult thing, not just hanging around entertaining or instructing."

~ John Holt

As I explain in the Courageous Homeschooling course, I have no doubt that having your own adult interests and hobbies is an essential part of keeping you sane while you homeschool, as well as being a brilliant way for the kids to learn.

If they see you tipping beads all over the table to create a Native Indian bracelet you'll soon see them trying it for themselves, writing their own patterns, helping you thread the beads, counting out the rows...

Hint Three

One other thing about the manner of your homeschool teaching.

Learning with your kids has to be **genuine**.

I can't think of anything more horrific than my well-meaning friend taking the children along a garden path of questions to get them to arrive at the answer she'd planted all along.

Children are not stupid.

They can smell **fake** as well as any adult.

Obviously, you aren't going to be interested in everything your children learn.

But you can try to make the things you do interesting to you too.

And one trick I used was to swing the projects and activities as much my way as I could get away with.

Which meant we did LOTS of crafts. I wanted to be enthusiastic too!

Hint Four

And another thing - you've spent hours and hours preparing a project.

You know it is going to be fabulous.

You've seen all the stuff everyone else is doing with their children.

You suggest it to your children.

And they aren't interested. Not in the slightest.

Motivation is, to put it mildly, zero.

All Catherine wanted to do was lie on the floor for three weeks!

I think that comes down to the fact that we still don't understand how children learn.

They don't have to be doing the things we think of as 'learning' in order to learn.

Staring into space is a very underrated educational tool!

You have to give plenty of time which is free and easy.

*"A child knows, and much better than anyone else, what he wants and needs to know **right now**, what his mind is ready and hungry for. If we help him, or just allow him, to learn that, he will remember it, use it, build on it.*

*If we try to make him learn something else, that **we think** is more important, the chances are that he won't learn it, or will learn very little of it, that he will soon forget most of what he learned, and what is worst of all, will before long lose most of his appetite for learning anything."*

~ John Holt

And we have to have the strength to fight off our inner dragons.

Leyli puts it very well:

"Don't panic and don't think that you have to do something to prove to the rest of the world that you are actually educating your son. it is the world around you who has to prove to YOU that what they are doing is right and better! :)))"

~ Leyli

I did come to an agreement with William and Catherine that they would try my suggestion for a morning and then we would decide to say NO.

But the point was - I hadn't killed the motivation because I had shown **respect**.

Hint Five

And that is the final point about being a homeschool teacher.

You have to respect what your child thinks and what their opinions are.

You have to LISTEN to them.

I am not saying that you need to do everything they say. That is straying into personal parenting styles which is not the point of this guide and entirely up to you.

But RESPECT is essential if you are going to keep your child motivated because they know that what they say matters.

You are listening. They do have a say.

"I tend to change the focus. It depends on the day. Sometimes that may mean taking a few minutes (or longer) and just letting people play. Sometimes it means changing the environment; for example, take the Math from the dining room table and do it under a shady tree in the yard.

Homeschooling is about redefining education anyway so personally I have had to work on being more **flexible***. I have learned the work will get done but who says it has to be done on my schedule? I have found that if I work with them they are more likely to work with me."*

~ Tobias

And look at this advice Dayna gave for how to avoid battles in your homeschool:

"I change the way I'm teaching. I want my children to **love to learn***. Learning shouldn't be torture and painful. If you want them to be life-time learners, you've got to let them do what interests them. When they want to learn, they will learn, and you won't have to make them do anything. They'll be inspired and excited.*

Find **their passion** *and talents, then you'll have to make them stop!"*

~Dayna

"A gardener does not grow flowers; he tries to give them what he thinks they need and they grow by themselves." ~ John Holt

Part Three

Dealing with Motivation Problems
in your Homeschool

Chapter Ten:

Practical Ideas to help Avoid Battles with your Kids

Good news! There's a lot you can do to try and turn things round if you start having the odd run-in with the kids.

Re-jigging your schedule can really help.

If you are anything like us, you've just about got it sussed, everyone's happy, then we grow up a bit, interests change, things move on...and we have to look at how to make our week work better ...yet again!

What about adding in a fun Friday? Only working in the mornings?

Here's an idea from Maria:
"I am not sure if it will be of any help, but we have

tried to use **our child's interests** for making material for her. *She likes Angry Birds, Star Wars, etc, and we have downloaded images and used them in the worksheets, we also have asked for permission of the parent's of her best friends to use their pictures, so she pre-writes looking at the pictures and explaining what they have been doing together. She likes animals, that are useful to introduce biomes and countries...*

We try that - as often as possible - **she has a connection to the activities** *and we think that is helping her to learn."*

~ Maria

I set up the **Courageous Homeschooling Facebook Group** so that we could help support each other through the ups and downs of our homeschooling days.

Having someone else who knows exactly what you are going through can help you re-think where you might be going wrong and what you need to change.

Here's a few typical exchanges in the group:

Help please!

"**Desperate** *for enlightenment. My kid* **refuses** *to do any work. Today Friday, we are still working on Monday work. I keep telling him that this is his job. It is OK not to like it but he still has to do it. So...I'm very frustrated.. Anyone have similar problems?"*

~ Thais

"Have been here with mine. Still debate with myself the need to finish tasks versus any learning is learning - and actually wanting to breed a love of learning! Very tricky when they aren't interested in anything.

*We now try to **get out more** and do more **hands-on arty stuff.**"*

~ Mandy

*"Hello! For us it took many months to get it to work....It has not been easy and we still have a way to go, but now it is really much easier and better... there are no fights and when I see that things start to get a little bit rocky I ask our child if she needs a **break.***

*We use lots of **positive encouragement**. Ah! For us it was important too, to have a routine, for a period we "worked" a little bit every single day (weekends too), now we have a "just" **fun learning day** (dropping what she dislikes) and one day off... Good luck!"*

~ Maria

"HANG on in there! Some weeks it can be nearly impossible then suddenly you see something working and you seem to forget all the difficult times. We almost gave up a month or so ago, but now everything is getting better."

~ Samantha

*"For my son, the situation was the same, no interest in school work, yelling matches, nagging, frustration. I finally researched **delight led learning** and we became **unschoolers**. Now my job is*

observing interests and providing resources.

*I act more as a **facilitator** of his learning. We go to the library, the zoo, art classes, I buy books or video games that inspire creativity, we watch cooking shows together, and he told me we should learn to cook together this summer."*

~ Lisa

Help please!

"We're doing animal extinction, covering dinosaurs, woolly mammoth etc,, Mine starts off well but loses interest and the work just sits there, it can be frustrating,,,"

~ Kaymeg

"(Kaymeg, just a suggestion but my daughter) Jayne loves dinosaurs, we have started doing a lapbook on them, we do so much a day or even leave it for a week, there are different things she can add to them, photos, drawings, writing, and making fossils. So much fun as it incorporates different topics.
*What is your little one's favorite topic? Work around that topic with your subjects. eg. There are 20 TREX eggs 4 hatch how many are left? That sort of thing. Might help to keep their **interest alive**."*

~ Sylvia

"Maybe we can take pics of wildlife and research its habitat etc..."

~ Kaymeg

*"That would be a **great idea** especially as the nicer weather is coming."*

~ Sylvia :)

Help please!

"I just don't feel confident that he's learning basic Math and English. I have also got him a journal recently so he can start journaling about his life on a Narrow boat. He's a bit reluctant to write atm but I'm hoping he will take to it. I'm going through a crisis of confidence atm"
~ Rachel

*"Rachel does he like computers? We set up a blog for our daughter, we use this to blog her journey, add photos of her art and I've also set up lessons on there for her. A lot is research. She is only 9 but she loves it. **Don't feel guilty.**"*
~ Sylvia

*"Hi Sylvia, yes he has a tablet and he did want a blog at one point but he's gone off that idea for some reason, so I gave him the option to do a blog or a journal and to my utter amazement he picked to write a journal with paper and pencil. **I'm thrilled** as his handwriting needs work as does his spelling. Maybe I'm not such a bad homeschooler as I thought lol xx"*
~ Rachel

*"There you go, you gave him the choice and you accepted it, you are definitely not a bad homeschooler, **listening to him** is a big step that they don't have at school. If he decides he does want a blog at a later stage, then let him research and set it up himself. How old is your son? Ask him if he wants to make the journal into a lapbook, this is another way of learning without them thinking it is learning."*
~ Sylvia

Suggestions from my Facebook fans:

*"Go out together and have a day off. Be **flexible** and **patient**."*
~ Haidar

*"I've learned over the years, that the work will get done. I **don't stress** about it. Everyone has bad days. You have to choose your battles. Some of our bad days have turned out to be our best."*
~ Sharon

*"If it is just the odd lesson here and there... I've offered them an alternative and **asked them** what 'they' preferred to do... **swap a lesson around** etc or **delay** it an hour or two. Hope this helps xx"*
~ Lynn

*"Take a **break** from "school". Learning happens in many ways and it doesn't have to look like "school." Find what their interests are and pursue that."*
~ Gina

*"Make sure the work isn't too hard or too easy. Just because something is supposed to be their "**grade level**" doesn't mean it is the best fit for your kiddo."*
~ Tracie

*"Let them **take a day off**! If learning isn't shoved down their throats like at public school, they will*

love learning! My kids rarely complain about projects or lessons."

~ Rachel

*"My Kindergartener does this all the time... I can't threaten to send him back to public school because he has never been. Besides, he'd probably want to go because his friends are there! We **take days off**. If I get too stressed about it I may want to quit myself."*

~ Jessica

*"Sometimes it is as easy as asking "why" and listening. There are fun ways to "cure" my hand or leg hurts, I'm hungry, I can't sit anymore. Sometimes their brains are focused on a much **bigger issue**."*

~ Tanya

*"Mine are 15, and 17 year old boys. I have a "**make a Deposit**" jar in our classroom. When they don't do their work, or talk back to me, they put $1 in the jar. So far I have $50."*

~ Sharon

*"To motivate Daisy age nine I had a chat with her and we agreed to have a box of **small prizes** maybe a skipping rope or a book or a comic, jigsaw puzzle, fun pens pencil or erasers. Daisy would gain 5 points for each piece of work or activity....reading, page in a work book or a work sheet, tending her vegetables, dance practice, a craft activity, making lunch....then once a week she would add up her points and choose something that we had placed an agreed point value on....**she***

loved this *and looked forward to spending her points each week."*

~ Susanne

"We run a **commendations** *policy too, 1 for every breakthrough or excellent behavior in specific settings and have a reward trip every 10, maybe to the cinema or theater etc."*

~ Sheila x

Chapter 11:
Motivation And Exams

What are you going to do about homeschooling and exams?

You'll see at the end of this book that some of us are questioning whether we should have to force our kids down this route.

The problem for homeschoolers is that you may well feel that you have already fought the system by taking your kids out of school, but you can't fight **the way the world works**.

After all, exams, sadly, are the rule-of-thumb markers which society uses to **judge people**.

And it is probably true that most homeschooling families do take the academic path.

That makes the **responsibility** and burden of **expectation** on you, as the homeschool parent, much heavier.

Even more so if you feel your kids results are a reflection of your homeschool 'success'.

So how are you going to deal with motivating your kids to get through them?

Now, don't panic!

Many homeschool co-ops offer classes which teach an extensive variety of subjects, easily covering the basics (Math, sciences, English, and history) as well as electives (art, drama, computer skills, personal finance, study skills, etc.)

And there are always tutors, on-line courses, and part-time study options.

But if, like us, you go down the **DIY route**, it makes it even more vital to get the **motivational relationship right**, because it will give you an opportunity to talk to your teen and see if they are prepared to put themselves through the hoops.

And, although I'm not saying that you will necessarily be able to use homeschooling to make **all** exams **fun**, together you may well be able to find ways to make them more interesting than they would have been!

Look at this inspiring story from Sheelagh:

"Just wanted to say...the stories of individual

*successes are so encouraging - they help the uncertain parent feel that **this homeschool adventure is achievable** and that good results don't have to be sacrificed just because we believe our children are better off being at home.*

My 16yr old dyslexic son just received his second batch of results. Last year he got an A* for Biology, an A for Physics, and Bs for Human Biology and Religious Studies. Today he added 2A*s for Math and Chemistry and 2As for Geography and English Language. I am over the moon with the A for his English because of his difficulties...

It was a real achievement for him.

My daughter is 14 and a little more suited to academic work. She loves exams and holding her back for two years would have been pointless... Besides the two of them worked together if they were stuck, revised together and tested each other... It worked well for both of them. She got her second batch of results today adding 5A*s and 1A to her previous 2A*s, 1A and 1B from last year.

*Both of them were **self taught** from textbooks. I consider myself to be more of a **facilitator of education** rather than a teacher at this stage.... Most of my time is taken up teaching my younger children.*

*I hope this is **encouraging** for some people starting the exam adventure. It is daunting at first, but not as tricky as it seems. I hope it doesn't seem as if I am boasting of my children's achievements... I tell the story mainly to encourage others. Our homeschool journey started to give our children a Christian education and many people thought we* *would end up depriving our children of academic opportunities. I am delighted to prove those cynics wrong."*

~ Sheelagh

Sheelagh's story shows that it is quite possible that when it comes to exams your child does the teaching **largely for themselves**.

That's exactly what our son William did, and it has taken him all the way to Oxford University.

So you may not have to **teach** exams at all!

Which removes a lot of potential problems on the motivation front.

But obviously not everyone is going to be as lucky as this!

Depending on how your child learns, some of us will definitely need to become very 'hands-on.'

So if we think that we want our children to get exams we're going to need to understand **what gets kids motivated** in order to succeed.

Which is why it is crucial you read the next part on what motivation is!

I must say it wasn't until I came to write this book

that I realized I had fallen into the common parent trap.

Even after all this time I hadn't fully understood what makes children motivated.

Reading Dennis Bumgarner's **free** book: **'***Motivating your intelligent but unmotivated teenager***'** changed all that.

I strongly recommend you read it too.

Here is the link:

http://behaviorcoach.com/EbookMotivatingVer3.pdf

It is a mind blower.

And the lessons he teaches us can help you with the biggest danger you face when you start homeschooling: motivation.

Just think how many young people are **switched off** by the system....so it is not your child's fault if they call time and refuse to jump.

This last section of the book is largely based on Bumgarner's ideas which I have adapted to homeschool. They will help you if you are struggling with getting your unmotivated homeschool teen on-side.

Chapter Twelve:

What is Motivation?

For over thirty years, Dennis Bumgarner has been counseling parents whose highly intelligent son or daughter is not doing what is necessary for academic success.

The reason so many parents turn to him is because:

*"Their (adolescent's) priorities are mixed-up, or they are not taking school seriously, they don't understand the **importance of education**, or they **lack motivation** to complete their work.*

You are not only frustrated; you are worried, perhaps heartsick. Knowing the relationship between academic success and eventual life satisfaction, you are anxious that your children will forever be behind life's eight-ball....

*It is not just grades that have you worried – **it is their life**."*

~ Dennis Bumgarner

Those worries about letting your children down are ones I have heard from most homeschoolers.

"I felt lost. That we never do anything and I am a failure."

~ Kirsty

It is the fear that strikes to the heart of homeschooling.

Dennis can help us.

He points out that most parents **misunderstand motivation**.

I can't do his thoughts justice here and I am going to make an assumption.

If you want to really understand how motivation works, you need to read his free book (I know - I said that before!)

I will, though, summarize briefly what he says so we can think about it from a **homeschooling** point of view.

The most important lesson I learned was that most parents (including Rob and me!) have never really understood what causes a child to **want** to do something.

That reminds me of the School Principal who announced that despite all her years teaching - she still had **no real idea** what made all the children she taught learn to read.

We think it is down to us, as homeschooling parents, to **get** our child motivated.

Dennis likens it to thinking we can sort-of **inject motivation** into our young person by what **we** do.

Let's look at this a bit more and stick with the reading example.

When we were homeschooling William, teaching him to read was so easy I don't remember trying.

With Catherine, we did everything we could think of – and more.

We tried not only all the different methods but also the usual motivational tools – praise, encouragement – I do believe there was a bit of bribery thrown in there too!

Nothing worked.

I remember Catherine announcing loudly in the library:

"Books are boring."

As you can imagine, exactly the sort of thing in public which is NOT music to a homeschool Mom's ears!

I gave up and handed her over to her grandma, who had homeschooled me along with most of my brothers.

I asked Mom recently (now age 96) how she had done it.

She said it was extremely difficult but that the secret she had eventually discovered was a pesky Gaul called **Asterix**.

The interesting thing is that *Asterix,* for those who know it, is really *not* the sort of book you would lay down for an early years reading curriculum.

It is far too complex and the joy comes from understanding the layers of meaning hidden in a single word.

But Catherine decided she wanted to read it, she chose the book; she struggled through, and she became as she is today...an avid reader.

The motivation was clearly internal; up to that point, whatever we had done to try and affect it, all our homeschooling motivational tactics added up to zero.

I have to say that Catherine didn't start reading until she was nearly eight and a half.

That's a long wait for homeschooling parents!

Luckily, Rob and I felt the most important goal was that she enjoyed reading **in the end** and quite frankly up to then she just wasn't ready to read; she was still enjoying *being read to* – and why shouldn't she?

It is only school that lays down the timetable – they know that's just taken from a statistical mean, but with the best will in the world they simply don't have time to wait until everyone is ready.

Maybe that's one of the reasons why so many children stop reading when they become adults.

In any case, Dennis' words are of fundamental importance to us homeschoolers.

Because he's saying that even if you try your very hardest and make all the effort in the world, you still can't necessarily get the motivation cog starting to spin.

This is such a big revelation to most of us that Bumgarner has to get us to see the truth of it by unpicking the assumptions which many of us make about how to motivate young people.

Chapter Thirteen:

Common Motivational Mistakes

Bumgarner is addressing here the problems you need to think about if your entering a tough battle zone with your teen over exams.

You need to read this if your teen doesn't want to do exams and doesn't see any point in them.

That's a nightmare homeschool scenario in homeschooling terms because you have to teach them!

So it is massively useful to see the mistakes you are likely to fall into so you can avoid the minefield.

Mistake One

First among these is that many parents think you need to encourage your child to get motivated by lots of **cheer leading** and what Dennis calls: *rah-rah*.

Definitely guilty as charged!

I love cheer leading. So this is something I would find very hard *not* to do.

Look at this rather chilling sentence:

*"For our present purposes, it is useful to know this: the reaction to this kind of over-enthusiastic cheer leading, especially for people who are demoralized or disheartened, is actually **demotivating**.*

*Because the person you are trying to motivate with these efforts doesn't believe the positive things being said about him, it is not only not motivating, it makes him feel **guilty**."*

~ Dennis Bumgarner

Thanks Dennis! Now I have started to think about it I can see that we know, as adults, that you only really like someone giving you praise if you believe you **deserve** it.

Otherwise, the words wash over you.

Worse, as Bumgarner points out, if you keep on

fruitlessly cheer leading, you appear so out of touch with the way your young person feels about themselves that it makes them feel you aren't **listening** to them.

Mistake Two

The second big motivational mistake that many parents make, according to Bumgarner, is hoping that by using rewards or punishments you can get the job done.

Bumgarner says:

*"Most parents know (or think they know) what motivates **them** and believe...that it will work with their teenagers, and are puzzled when it does not.*

*They have a strong but unfounded faith in the power of **incentives** and/or **punishments** to motivate their adolescents."*

Note the hammer blow contained in the words: *'unfounded faith'*!!!

He says there is **little evidence** that doing this gets you where you want to go.

Remember, Bumgarner is speaking about teenagers who are already de-motivated and he is assuming that you wouldn't be reading his book if your attempts are working.

You and your partner will decide between yourselves what you feel comfortable with in your homeschool and if it works....well, that's your choice.

In our homeschool, the children were motivated. They wanted to learn.

So I never went on to give 'extra' rewards for doing their work well like giving them extra gaming time or taking them to watch a movie or ....anything much at all!

What a bad parent I was.

William and Catherine didn't even really get pocket money!

But if your children like getting **gold stars**, why not?

It is certainly an age old remedy and one schools make full use of.

And if it makes your kids motivated and wanting to learn - full marks to you.

As to the other side of the coin - withholding privileges, forfeits etc.

Well we never went down that road. We didn't need to.

But you and your partner will decide between yourselves what you feel comfortable with and if it works....well, that's your choice.

Here's a few homeschool insights from my Facebook fans:

"All work must be complete or **no privileges** *are given (computer, phone, games). It is always their choice to finish their work or not, but they know the consequence.*

Of course we school year around and some days require more time and diligence than others, but we have plenty of off time to play!"

~ Denise

"I've learned over the years, that the **work will get done***. I don't stress about it. Everyone has bad days. You have to choose your battles.*

Some of our bad days, have turned out to be our best. My boys are in 10th, and 12th grades."

~ Sharon

"My oldest daughter (now 20 yrs old and recently married) is extremely stubborn and unfortunately she has learned most of her lessons about having to do school work in the school of hard knocks. Her refusal to do her work was not just an occasional thing, it was everyday.

I tried numerous different curriculums, teaching styles, etc without success. Finally, when it came to high school and grades, etc would really count for college, we sent her to **public high school***.*

She went 2 yrs before she realized the grass was

not greener on the other side of the fence and asked to come home. This is not always the best answer but for a chronic problem it is something to pray about."

~ Heather

*"I know from experience that when they get it once, they try it again and again....it is not about me being flexible, it is about the children getting to know the **rules**....*

Home schooling is anyways more flexible than school ... how much more flexible should it be when children don't want to do school work!?"

~ Maria

*"I've used the threat of sending mine back to public school but it doesn't always work so the other incentive is **take away TV etc.** until work is done.*

Seems to work *most of the time."*

~ Karen

Bumgarner is writing about when NOTHING works at all.

And it is an eye-opening lesson for me.

Personally, I **love** cheer leading

I think the world is a gray place without praise and encouragement and we could all do with being nicer to each other and appreciating each others achievements.

So it is a revelation that this isn't always the best way forward.

Mistake Three

Bumgarner says that we delude ourselves if we think we need to get motivated in order to **do** something.

He believes it is the other way round.

You get the motivation by DOING the thing.

"The key is not to try to get your teenager motivated (which has previously involved ineffective consequences and useless verbiage) but to instead do something different to try to get him to perform.

*Your concern is to get the desired behavior started, **not to change the mind of your teenager** (a difficult, if not impossible - but thankfully unnecessary – task.)"*

With first-hand experience of dealing with teenagers, I can't help but smile over the last bit!

Mistake Four

This was the biggest revelation of all to me and has enormous relevance to homeschooling.

Bumgarner says that saying your young person "lacks motivation" chimes with the belief that motivation lies within the individual.

Agh!!! I am so used to saying: '*William is very self-motivated.*'

In fact, it is taken as read among homeschoolers and all parents to talk about **self-motivation** and the **need to motivate** your child.

*"If, like most parents, you hold this belief, then you will attempt to **inject** your teenager with motivation, to get it inside him by any means necessary...*

*This is what happens when you try to get into the head of your teenager through **incessant lecturing**, or when you use punishments to attempt to trigger the motivational button inside him.*

*Since motivation is not a characteristic of an individual, these methods are virtually guaranteed to **fail**."*

~ Dennis Bumgarner

There is a bit of relief for homeschoolers here.

I don't think Bumgarner means we shouldn't do our best to think up as many activities as we can that go with the interests of our individual child.

But it is the **doing of those activities** which creates the motivation **within** the child.

Mistake Five

When I read the fifth mistake most parents make, I got really excited.

And **proud**.

Because when Bumgarner wrote this:

*"Truly motivational relationships are not those in which one of the members is in a **one-up** position, as when an authority directs the behavior of a subordinate.*

*Relationships which are motivational are **genuine partnerships**, where neither member lords power over the other."*

~ Dennis Bumgarner

That was exactly the sort of relationship I was trying to describe when I wrote earlier about what it is like to be a homeschool teacher.

I finally understand WHY what we had done had helped William and Catherine find their own motivation.

"We can best help children learn, not by deciding what we think they should learn and thinking of ingenious ways to teach it to them, but by making the world, as far as we can, accessible to them, paying serious attention to what they do, answering their questions -- if they have any -- and helping them explore the things they are most interested in."

~ John Holt

Chapter Fourteen:

How to Motivate a Switched-Off Teen

Dennis Bumgarner is a counseling expert who has made this his profession for the last 35 years.

So we can learn lots from him!

I'd love to encourage you to read his book. And I'd like to give you some suggestions for how to adapt his ideas to homeschooling.

Here is a brief summary of the important points he makes:

1.   Teenagers change their behavior which **then** affects the way they think (and not the other way round!)

2.   If you try to short-cut the process by hoping

that **punishments** will create the motivation you seek, your teenager is liable to duck. *"Bad feelings and unpleasant experiences tend to immobilize teenagers rather than spur them to action."* ~ Bumgarner

3. Research shows that teenagers are more likely to change if:

a) They discover something intrinsically good *for them* about the change they are making

b) They have decided *for themselves* they want to change (you can't force them to do so, however much sense it makes!)

c) Your relationship with your young person is **safe**, **accepting** and **empowering** so that your child can *"express any thought or emotion to you and you will accept it without evaluation or criticism."*

~ Bumgarner

The last point is particularly tough. It means you have to let them say what they feel and not what you **hoped** they'd say!

Bumgarner writes about how difficult this is for parents, because we want to teach, instruct and guide.

But I think we can all see the sense in what he was saying.

I HATE being given advice.

As the youngest of six children, it seems to be my

lot in life to be the one who gets stuck with hours of well-meaning advice about everything from how to boil potatoes (yes, really!) to looking after my own Mom.

Needless to say, those calls always leave me fuming.

It seems we are all good at giving advice.

"One of the rarest of human experiences is to be **truly listened to** *by another person...Few adolescents have experienced this with adults, who are oh so quick to tell kids what they need to do, thereby killing the very motivation they are trying to promote."*

~ Bumgarner

Look how this links with what John Holt says:

"Many parents...tell about their...children getting **furiously angry** *when their kind and loving parents, meaning only for the best, try to give them help they have not asked for."*

~ John Holt, *How Children Learn*

The point is we seek advice when we have decided we are **in need of** some – and not before!

Bumgarner points out that if you want someone to change, you have to **accept them as they are.**

He then goes on to explain that the change process, annoyingly, is not straightforward.

If your teen realizes for themselves that exams are a good idea, sadly you still aren't on the home straight.

Because they might change their minds!

Change in a teenager doesn't follow a logical path from *not* wanting to change to **wanting** to change.

Bother!

Instead it bounces around back and forth with a lot of indecisiveness in the middle.

I'm going to back off now, because he goes on to explain the five stages of change (pre-contemplation, contemplation, preparation, action and maintenance) and this is his field, not mine!

But I think I can add a few things to what Bumgarner says which will help, partly because his training has taught him things that homeschooling parents don't necessarily know.

Firstly, it is worth remembering that, although you are having these problems in homeschool, you might well have faced the same problems - or worse

- if you had sent your child to **public school**.

After all, Bumgarner isn't expecting me to have written this book – his hands are full enough already!

So don't blame yourself.

I'll borrow Bumgarner's words because I am certain they apply to you:

*"You are an **involved**, **committed** and **conscientious** parent. Your efforts are logical, reasonable and grounded in common sense. Your well-intentioned efforts to motivate your teenager are beyond all criticism except one: they haven't worked."*

~ Bumgarner

Secondly, Bumgarner is trained and we aren't.

So when it comes to the crucial part about listening to your child, **live the silence**.

When you are trying to find out what they think, it is really hard not to fill in the gaps!

Thirdly, **you can control your behavior, you cannot control your child's**.

The reality is you are one of the few punch bags that's round all day for your child to hit.

Could be that you are getting some pretty heavy stick from your child, who has no one else to take it out on.

And it is hard to admit, but it may be that your child is subconsciously trying to upset and provoke you.

Let's look at one of the traditional parental red rags: **getting up late**.

Even in our homeschool, I really struggled with this one when we hit the teen years.

Partly because, as a homeschooling parent, having the children in bed while everyone else is at school sounds like I'm not doing my 'job'.

With teenagers, it is easier to be reasonable and accept the research that proves that they need more sleep.

So it makes good sense to start the day later.

It gets harder when we have all 'agreed' the getting up time and..nothing happens.

It gets harder still when we have 'agreed' that owning our own alarm clock might help and...nothing happens.

The first knock at half past ten is okay, the second one quarter of an hour later is getting more difficult, the third one...hmmm beginning to fizz...the fourth one....oh no, lost it again!!!!

You know things are going wrong when every morning starts with a battle.

A battle which I was losing.

Because, apart from my blood pressure and the toxic atmosphere in the house (great way to start the day!), I wasn't succeeding in making any difference whatsoever to what time the day began.

So I decided to award myself **Victory Points** for *not* getting upset.

All that playing board games has come in at last!

The more I can knock with a cheery remark the more points I score.

Works a treat! Occasionally I pop into another room and do a high five.

Once again, you are back re-learning the truth of Bumgarner's words.

You can't **make** your child do what they don't want

to do.

But you can poison the house by trying.

So give yourself a reward – start counting Victory Points and stay as calm as you can!

What's more, I think you'll find Bumgarner's book a revelation.

His work has great implications for all homeschoolers, because he shows us:

1.   In the end, **motivation** and the desire to **change behavior** is **down to our children** and not us.

2.   We have a vital role to play in creating the **right relationship with our child** so that motivation can thrive.

3.   You can help your child change their behavior once you have got **them** to find out what **their own goals, beliefs and values are**.

He also says this:

"While enhanced academic performance seems to be an unalloyed positive development (improved grades, more privileges, better relationship with parents), this improvement comes at a cost (more time spent studying boring material, less time for fun).

*The teen may determine that **the cost** outweighs*

the potential benefit."

~ Bumgarner

And if, after all your best efforts, your teen decides they really don't want to do exams, you are going to have to step back.

Because the most important role you have in life is that of being a parent, not a teacher.

Battlefields and war zones are not the place to run a happy home!

Look at what Bumgarner says:

"When you push your adolescent to make a change he is unwilling or unprepared to make, he pushes back....What then ensues is the parent/child version of trench warfare during World War 1 – lots of noise, explosions, and damage, while the front lines remain unmoved."

~ Dennis Bumgarner

So you are going to have to accept the truth of what your teen says they want to do.

Because however well you teach, you won't get anywhere if your teen won't learn.

So you have to learn the art of acceptance.

That's tough.

And that boils down to trust.

I have always said that learning to **trust your child** is the hardest homeschooling lesson of all.

"All I am saying...can be summed up in two words - Trust Children. Nothing could be more simple - or more difficult. Difficult, because to trust children we must trust ourselves - and most of us were taught as children that we could not be trusted."

~ John Holt

And I like this one too:

"You have brains in your head. You have feet in your shoes. You can steer yourself any direction you choose. You're on your own. And you know what you know. And YOU are the one who'll decide where to go..."

~ Dr. Seuss

Just to prove that non-exam route isn't quite as scary as it sounds, I want to do a bit of mud-stirring in the last chapter.

Because it will really help on the motivation front if your mind is open to alternatives if your child really doesn't want to do them.

Chapter Fifteen:
Are Exams A Good Idea?

I think most of us start homeschooling and it doesn't even cross our mind to question whether our kids will take exams.

Of course they will.

After all, everyone else seems to!

So I want to sow a few seeds of doubt in your mind in case they apply to your child.

If you know right from the start your child just isn't suited to them it will save an enormous lot of heartache.

And you may also come to believe that the whole system sucks!

After all, we all know the truth behind this famous

115

quote:

Grades don't measure intelligence and age doesn't define maturity.

Look at what Lisa says:

*"Sometimes, a child can become inspired to learn by **having a part** in that learning. If they do not see any relevance to their life, they may shut down and give up in discouragement. Ultimately, the beauty of homeschool is the ability to **break free of the system** that says you have to learn A,B, and C and to tailor your child's learning and mentor them in a way that is meaningful to their real life and goals.*

*My feeling upon graduating public school was that I wish I could have gone back and **done High School differently**. I took so many classes because I had to and to get into college. If I could do it now, I would have taken less Math, which I hated, and would have taken more art and writing classes. I might have dabbled in acting or the chorus or in a music class. I feel I wasted a lot of time memorizing things for a test that I will never use and that I sort of missed out. Now, at almost 50 years old, I am inspired and am playing catch up. I am learning to paint and cross stitch and play the ukelele and drums. Homeschool has literally birthed a love of learning and a deep curiosity in me over the last several 9 years. I love it."*

~ Lisa

Let's start by looking at some of the research so you can see that it is not just me who thinks a lot of the curriculum-type stuff can be a killer.

Here's a really interesting blog post from Will Richardson, the international speaker and writer on education.

In it, he talks about the elephants in the classroom that we need to start talking about.

The first of these is:

*"For more than 75 years, studies have consistently found that only a **small fraction** of what is learned in the classroom is retained even a year after learning.*

*That's primarily because the curriculum and classroom work they experience has **little or no relevance** to students' real lives."*

~ Will Richardson

I would go further. I would say that we are expecting young people to do work that **isn't relevant** to most **adults**.

And it is certainly not relevant to where most teenager's heads are!

So that's a massive problem on the motivation front.

Look at this heart-felt plea:

"I don't want to learn in a classroom anymore. I want to travel and talk to people and learn that way.

I want to learn as I go, gathering knowledge and not being rigorously tested on it. I don't want to lose passion in the things I like because of the worry of **exams.**

I want to be fueled by snippets of knowledge I gain from people and be inquisitive. School has stolen my passion for the things I'm interested in and I hate it for that."

~ Anonymous

Of course, I'm not saying the teachers who wrote the curricula **mean** to put so many pupils off.

It is just a shame they seem to succeed so well in something they didn't intend!

Here's Will Richardson again:

"We know that most of our students are bored and disengaged in school. *According to a recent* <u>Gallup survey</u>, *only 32% of high school juniors reported that they were "involved and enthusiastic about school."*

Almost worse, only 17% said that they have fun in school, the same number that said they "get to do what they do best" in school."

~ Will Richardson

Perhaps it is something inherent in having to form a **committee** of well-intentioned people to draw up a syllabus rather than allowing one passionate person to let rip.

And of course there's the problem of trying to make things fair and produce something that can be rolled out across the country which all schools can deliver to groups of children in lesson-sized chunks.

Sarah really puts her finger on the **motivation problem** you face when you consider this truth:

*"All of our children have **different talents** or gifts...Some children will be gifted academically, but others will have a hard time with book work. Some will see beauty in every corner, while another has music filling his soul. One runs like the wind, another has a heart to serve mankind.*

How can we judge one gift to be more valuable than another? And how can we deny our child's gifts and try and stuff them in a box labeled Standardized Achievement?"

~ Sarah in *Homeschooling: A Patchwork of Days*

Our experience is that science subjects are great if you love **facts**. Sadly, not everyone does.

English – well, dissecting words is a well-known turn off. How many adults know – or care - what *modal verbs* or *iambic pentameters* are?

I always enjoy this quote from one of the most famous and well-loved childrens' authors, Michael Morpurgo, himself the possessor of a failed 11+, disappointing grades and the lowest College degree you can get:

"I would read to my Year Six children only those

stories I loved myself – and when I ran out of those I told my own. I told my story with total commitment, lived every word, and so they believed every word. I did not ask questions about it afterwards. I did not test them. I simply let them lose themselves in the story, in the music of the words. "

~ Michael Morpurgo

I'd love to have been one of the children in his class.

My own experience of being sent to High School confirms my belief that **school** and **studying for exams** often destroys children's enthusiasm – for life.

"These days, anyone whose real strengths lie outside the restricted field of academic work can find being at school a dispiriting experience and emerge from it wondering if they have any significant aptitudes at all."

~ Sir Ken Robinson

How are you going to motivate your child if they see you simply as an authority figure making them do something they don't want to do?

*"One of the essential problems for education is that most countries subject their schools to the **fast-food model of quality assurance** when they should be adopting the Michelin model instead.*

The future for education is not in standardizing

but in customizing; not in promoting groupthink and "deindividuation" but in cultivating the real depth and dynamism of human abilities of every sort."

~ Sir Ken Robinson

And look at this stark statement from Will Richardson:

"We know that **deep, lasting learning** requires **conditions** that **schools** and classrooms simply **were not built for**....(and that) we're not assessing many of the things that **really matter** for future success."

~ Will Richardson

That's a massive conclusion.

And it gives us heart.

Because it proves that homeschooling gives us a unique opportunity to allow our children to discover their true talents and abilities.

Look at all the people who have succeeded **without exams**.

Let's take comfort from reminding ourselves of a few famous 'failures':

* Richard Branson's net worth is said to be roughly $4.9 billion. He never completed High School, and dropped out at 16 years of age.

* Steve Jobs bailed out of Reed College to

become the father of all things Apple.

* After failing every subject except English, Al Pacino quit his New York High School to pursue acting.

So Billy Connolly is just one among many famous people who gets the last laugh at those who think the academic route is the only way to success!

You don't **have to** follow the exam route when you homeschool teens.

They may find their own path to success much better without them.

And you also have to agree with Charlotte Mason the truth in these words:

"The question is not, - how much does the youth know? when he has finished his education - but how much does he care?"

~ Charlotte Mason

Think of all the qualities exams don't measure and rejoice.

*"The people who create these tests and score them do not know that...you can play a **musical** instrument...or that you can **dance**...or **paint** a picture...They do not know that your **friends** can count on you to be there for them or that your **laughter** can brighten the dreariest day."*

~ Rachel Tomlinson, School Principal

Your main aim has to be that your child is happy, creative and fulfilled in life.

That's something no formal exam is designed to measure.

But it is where homeschooling scores the highest marks.

Conclusion:

Good Luck!

Finally, homeschooling is all about helping each other.

If you would like more **practical help** on how to go about building a homeschool that works for all of you, I have used my experience as one of the very few second generation homeschooling families to write a **How to Homeschool e-book**.

It walks you through in **13 practical steps** how to build a successful homeschool.

You can also come and join us on the free **Courageous Homeschooling course**. The course has 21 daily lessons which take just 10 minutes a day and an exclusive Facebook Group.

"Just a note to say how fantastic Sonya's free Courageous Homeschooling course is, if you haven't done it is a MUST! It takes 5-10 minutes a

day and is SO uplifting to the soul. I've been homeschooling for a year and after yesterday's and today's posts I feel a different person...Thank you for making a difference to our lives."

~ Sheila

You'll find a beautiful *Homeschool Journal* where you can write down the things which inspire you, work out your homeschooling goals and record the highlights of your homeschooling journey.

My website at *www.homeschool-activities.com* is the place to go to find free resources, curriculum advice, fun learning activities for all the key subjects like Science, Math and English, art and craft ideas, and general help and advice on all aspects of homeschool.

You can also subscribe to a free *Monthly Activities newsletter*, which is full of activities for **all ages** based around fascinating themes like Art, Science, Math and Crafts. You'll also find lots of free printables, interesting websites, recommended books, even recipes and gifts!

Meanwhile, your support posse is waiting. You can become part of a community which is ready to share your worries, fears and triumphs.

The *Courageous Homeschooling Facebook Group* is the place to come to share what you are up to each day and where we give each other help and support and take heart from each other.

And you'll love getting daily inspiration and help on my main *Facebook* page with over 10,000 fans.

Thank you for reading! I do hope you found this book useful.

I wish you much joy on your homeschooling journey.

Best wishes

Sonya

PS If you enjoyed this book, please consider telling your friends, your homeschool group or posting a short review on Amazon.

It would be really encouraging for me to know that this book has helped you in some way.

Made in the USA
Lexington, KY
25 October 2017